cheesecakes

RYLAND
PETERS
& SMALL
LONDON NEW YORK

cheesecakes

Maxine Clark Photography by Martin Brigdale

First published in Great Britain in 2003
by Ryland Peters & Small
Kirkman House
12–14 Whitfield Street
London W1T 2RP
www.rylandpeters.com

10 9 8 7 6 5 4 3 2 1

Printed in China

ISBN 1 84172 487 4

A CIP record for this book is available
from the British Library.

Senior Designer Steve Painter
Commissioning Editor
Elsa Petersen-Schepelern
Editor Kathy Steer
Production Patricia Harrington
Art Director Gabriella Le Grazie
Publishing Director Alison Starling

Food Stylists Maxine Clark,
Bridget Sargeson
Stylist Helen Trent
Indexer Hilary Bird

Author's acknowledgements
Special thanks go to my sister Jacks
for help with recipe testing. Thanks
to Martin and Helen for producing
wonderful photographs yet again, with
Bridget, who will probably never eat a
cheesecake again. My lovely editor, Elsa,
should get any blame for weight gain
when using this book – it was her idea.

Notes
• All spoon measurements are level
unless otherwise specified.
• All eggs are medium unless otherwise
specified. Uncooked or partly cooked
eggs should not be served to the very
young, the very old, those with
compromised immune systems or
to pregnant women.
• Before baking, weigh or measure all
ingredients exactly and prepare baking
tins or sheets.
• Ovens should be preheated to the
specified temperature. Recipes in this
book were tested in several kinds of
oven – all work slightly differently. I
recommend using an oven thermometer
and consulting the maker's handbook for
special instructions.

**Fat content of cheeses
used in this book**

All cheeses labelled 'Light' or 'Extra-
Light' have added stabilizers and
although they reduce the calories,
the texture in cooked cheesecakes
may be different when substituted for
the higher fat version.

• Cottage Cheese (white, with a
knobbly texture and slight acidity) has
1.8 per cent fat.
• Quark (white, soft and smooth, made
from skimmed milk, slight acidity) –
variable but always low.
• Fromage Frais (a white, soft, fresh curd
cheese originally from France) – there are
three types: 0.1 per cent fat, 4 per cent
fat and 8 per cent fat. The last one is
most used in cooking.
• Ricotta (made from the recooked
whey left over from making cheese) is
white, with a slightly granular texture –
14 per cent fat.
• Philadelphia Full-Fat Soft Cheese (white
and creamy smooth) has 24 per cent fat.
• Curd Cheese or Medium-Fat Soft
Cheese (similar to cream cheese, but
paler in colour and a slightly lower fat
content) – variable fat levels.
• Mascarpone (an Italian cream cheese,
pale yellow and creamy, with a distinctive
rich creamy flavour) has 40 per cent fat.
• Cream Cheese (pale yellow in colour,
soft and buttery) has 45 per cent fat.

contents

perfect for pudding ...

Say the word 'cheesecake' and most people will sigh with pleasure and start to recall their favourites. We see cheesecakes everywhere now, from coffee bars to supermarket shelves, but the best are always homemade.

My first taste of a real baked cheesecake was on childhood trips to Harrogate in Yorkshire many years ago. They were thick and dense and incredibly rich. Then I tasted real Jewish cheesecake in Petticoat Lane in London – this was a revelation! I was converted, and started to collect and try all sorts of recipes.

Cheesecake was particularly popular in Britain in the '70s, and always seen as something rather exotic – it came from faraway places like Italy, America and Eastern Europe. In America of course, immigrants from all over the world contributed their own twist to the art, whether it be in the type of cheese used, or the added ingredients.

That said, baked cheesecake is always best served with coffee. Nowadays, we forget that these baked cheesecakes came earlier than the lighter, uncooked cheesecakes set with gelatine, which were seen as a quick and easy alternative, and could look very glamorous indeed. Gelatine-set cheesecakes became the perfect conclusion to a dinner party and still are today – they look spectacular, are relatively simple to make and taste wonderful.

Whether baked or set, cheesecakes are a firm favourite in the Western world, and the best are made at home – especially if it's one of these ...

making cheesecake bases
shortcrust pastry

This is the classic method for making short and crumbly shortcrust pastry. It is made with half butter and half lard – the butter for colour and flavour and cooking fat for shortness. If you have cool hands, the hand method is best as it will incorporate more air than in a food processor. If you have hot hands, the food processor is a blessing! The quantities of water added vary according to such things as the humidity of the flour – always add less than it says, you can always add more if it is dry, but once it is a sticky mess, it could prove disastrous!

basic shortcrust pastry

250 g plain flour, plus extra
for dusting

a pinch of salt

50 g lard or white cooking fat,
chilled and cut into small pieces

75 g unsalted butter, chilled
and cut into small pieces

2–3 tablespoons iced water

**Makes about 400 g, enough to
line the base of a 23 cm fluted
flan tin, or 10 loose-based
tartlet tins, 10 cm diameter**

Sift the flour and salt into a large bowl. Add the lard
and butter, and using your fingertips, rub it in until
the mixture resembles fine breadcrumbs. Stir in
enough chilled water, about 2–3 tablespoons, to
produce a firm dough.

Transfer the dough to a lightly floured work surface
and knead lightly. Shape the dough into a flattened
ball, wrap in clingfilm and chill for at least 30 minutes
before rolling out.

To make the pastry in a food processor, sift the flour
and salt into the processor. Add the lard and butter
and process for 30 seconds until the mixture
resembles very fine breadcrumbs. Pour in
2 tablespoons water and pulse for 10 seconds. The
dough should start to come together in large lumps.
If not, add 1 tablespoon water and pulse again. As
soon as the dough forms a large lump, transfer to
a lightly floured work surface and knead lightly.
Proceed as above.

Note for both recipes If using a food processor, do
not overprocess, otherwise the pastry will be tough.

rich shortcrust pastry

250 g plain flour, plus extra
for dusting

½ teaspoon salt

125 g unsalted butter, chilled
and cut into small pieces

2 egg yolks

2–3 tablespoons iced water

**Makes about 400 g, enough to
line the base of a 23 cm fluted
flan tin, or 10 loose-based
tartlet tins, 10 cm diameter**

Sift the flour and salt into a large bowl. Add the
butter and, using your fingertips, rub it in until the
mixture resembles fine breadcrumbs. Stir in the egg
yolks mixed with at least 2 tablespoons iced water
to make a firm but malleable dough.

Transfer the dough to a lightly floured work surface
and knead until smooth. Shape the dough into a
flattened ball, wrap in clingfilm and chill for at least
30 minutes before rolling out.

To make the pastry in a food processor, sift the flour
and salt into the processor. Add the butter and
process for 30 seconds until the mixture resembles
fine breadcrumbs. Pour in the egg yolks mixed with
at least 2 tablespoons iced water and pulse for
10 seconds. The dough should start to come together
in lumps. If not, add 1 tablespoon water and pulse
again. As soon as the dough forms a large lump,
transfer to a lightly floured work surface and knead
into a firm but malleable dough. Proceed as above.

Variation To make Sweet Rich Shortcrust Pastry,
add 2 tablespoons icing sugar with the flour.

biscuit bases

biscuit crumb base

100 g digestive biscuits

50 g butter

50 g caster sugar

Makes enough to line the base of a 20 cm tin or dish

Put the biscuits in a food processor and blend until crumbs form. Alternatively, put the biscuits in a plastic bag and crush finely with a rolling pin.

Melt the butter and sugar in a small saucepan over gentle heat. Stir in the crumbs and use at once.

chocolate crumb base

175 g chocolate-coated digestives, chocolate chip cookies or chocolate bourbon biscuits

75 g butter

25 g soft brown sugar

Makes enough to line the base of a 20 cm tin or dish

Put the biscuits in a food processor and blend until crumbs form. Alternatively, put the biscuits in a plastic bag and crush finely with a rolling pin.

Melt the butter and sugar in a small saucepan over gentle heat. Stir in the crumbs and use at once.

nutty biscuit crumb base

75 g digestive biscuits

50 g butter

50 g caster sugar

25 g chopped toasted nuts, such as hazelnuts, walnuts or almonds*

Makes enough to line the base of an 20 cm tin or dish

Put the biscuits in a food processor and blend until crumbs form. Alternatively, put the biscuits in a plastic bag and crush finely with a rolling pin.

Melt the butter and sugar in a small saucepan over gentle heat. Stir in the crumbs and chopped nuts and use at once.

*Note To toast nuts, put them in a dry frying pan and stir over gentle heat until starting to colour all over. Watch them closely, because they burn easily. Alternatively, put the nuts on a baking sheet and cook in a preheated oven at 190°C (375°F) Gas 5 until lightly coloured.

oven-baked cheesecakes

Baked cheesecake mixtures contain whole eggs, which add lightness to the mixture and cook to set the cake. Classic American and Italian cheesecakes are made this way and have a completely different texture from a set cheesecake. Some are deep and some shallow, but both have a tendency to crack during cooking, so don't worry if this happens to you.

This is the real thing – a dense, rich cheesecake with a crunchy biscuit base. Serve with your favourite cup of coffee and imagine yourself in a New York deli!

traditional new york cheesecake

Base

200 g digestive biscuits

100 g unsalted butter

75 g caster sugar

Filling

150 g unsalted butter

170 g caster sugar

4 large eggs, beaten

30 g plain flour

finely grated zest and juice of 1 large unwaxed lemon

½ teaspoon vanilla essence

675 g full-fat soft cheese (Philadelphia), at room temperature

60 ml milk

Topping

425 ml sour cream

1 tablespoon icing sugar

freshly squeezed juice of 1 lemon

a springform cake tin, 23 cm diameter, greased

a baking sheet

Serves 10–12

To make the crumb base, put the biscuits in a food processor and process until fine crumbs form. Alternatively, put the biscuits in a large plastic bag and finely crush them with a rolling pin. Melt the butter in a small saucepan over gentle heat, then stir in the crumbs and sugar. Spread the crumb mixture over the base of the prepared cake tin, pressing down lightly. Stand the tin on a baking sheet and cook in a preheated oven at 190°C (375°F) Gas 5 for 8–10 minutes. Remove from the oven and let cool.

Reduce the temperature to 160°C (325°F) Gas 3. To make the filling, put the butter and sugar in a large bowl and, using a wooden spoon or electric hand mixer, beat until pale and fluffy. Gradually beat in the eggs. Mix in the flour, lemon zest, lemon juice and vanilla. Put the soft cheese in a separate bowl and, using a wooden spoon or electric hand mixer, beat until smooth. Gently beat in the milk, then gradually beat in the butter and sugar mixture. Spoon the mixture over the crumb base and level the surface. Bake in the preheated oven for 1½ hours.

To make the topping, put the sour cream, icing sugar and lemon juice in a large bowl and, using a wooden spoon or electric hand mixer, beat lightly. Chill in the refrigerator until required.

Remove the cheesecake from the oven and increase the temperature to 190°C (375°F) Gas 5. Pour the topping over the surface of the cheesecake, level and return to the oven for a further 10 minutes or until set. Turn off the oven, leave the door ajar and let the cheesecake cool in the oven to prevent it cracking. Alternatively, transfer it to a wire rack, invert a large bowl over the cake, then let cool. Chill the cheesecake for 2 hours before serving.

I have been making this cheesecake since I started cooking at the tender age of eight—it used to be my *pièce de résistance*! Blending the sugar with large strips of lemon zest transfers the essential oils to the sugar and gives a wonderful aroma to the tart. Use cottage cheese instead of cream cheese to give a lighter texture. Mascarpone Cream or Lemon Syllabub Cream (page 63) would be delicious with this cheesecake.

simple lemon cheese tart

1 recipe Sweet Rich Shortcrust Pastry (page 9, see Variation), at room temperature

plain flour, for dusting

Filling

1 unwaxed lemon

75 g caster sugar

350 g full-fat soft cheese (Philadelphia)

1 large egg, plus 3 egg yolks

2 teaspoons vanilla essence

a loose-based tart tin, 23 cm diameter

baking parchment and ceramic baking beans or rice

Serves 4–6

Roll out the pastry on a lightly floured work surface and use to line the tart tin. Prick the base with a fork, then chill or freeze for 15 minutes. Cut out a large piece of baking parchment to fit the tin, use to line the pastry case, then fill with ceramic baking beans or rice. Alternatively, line the pastry case with crumpled foil. Bake in a preheated oven at 190°C (375°F) Gas 5 for 10 minutes. Remove the baking parchment and beans or foil and return to the oven for a further 10 minutes. Let cool.

Using a vegetable peeler, remove the zest from the lemon leaving behind any white pith, then squeeze the juice. Put the lemon zest and sugar in a food processor or blender and process until the sugar and lemon zest mixture looks damp.

Add the lemon juice and process again (the lemon zest should have completely dissolved in the sugar), then add the soft cheese, the whole egg, egg yolks and vanilla essence and blend until smooth. Pour the mixture into the pastry case.

Bake the tart in a preheated oven at 190°C (375°F) Gas 5 for 25 minutes or until just set and lightly browned on top. Remove from the oven and let cool. Serve at room temperature.

Delicious for a summer lunch, this rich cheesecake is perfect for any special occasion. For best results, make sure all the filling ingredients are at room temperature.

ricotta and muscatel raisin cheesecake

Pastry

225 g fine polenta

75 g plain flour, plus extra for dusting

125 g caster sugar

55 g toasted pine nuts

175 g unsalted butter, diced

2 large egg yolks

Filling

75 g large Muscatel raisins

2–3 tablespoons Vin Santo or Marsala wine

500 g ricotta cheese

500 g full-fat soft cheese

240 ml sour cream

4 large eggs, separated

125 g caster sugar

2 teaspoons vanilla essence

freshly grated nutmeg

salt

a springform cake tin, 23 cm diameter, greased and base-lined

baking parchment and ceramic baking beans or rice

Serves 8–10

To make the pastry, put the polenta, flour, sugar, pine nuts and butter in a food processor and blend, in short bursts, until the mixture resembles coarse breadcrumbs. Add the egg yolks and process until the dough forms a ball. Wrap in clingfilm and chill for 1 hour.

Roll out the pastry on a sheet of lightly floured, greaseproof paper to about 7 mm thickness and carefully use to line the tin. Chill for 5 minutes. Cut out a large piece of baking parchment to fit the tin, put it on top of the pastry case, then fill with ceramic baking beans or rice. Alternatively, line the pastry case with crumpled foil. Bake in a preheated oven at 180°C (350°F) Gas 4 for 10 minutes. Remove the baking parchment and beans or foil and return to the oven for a further 10 minutes. Let cool.

To make the filling, put the raisins in a small bowl, add the Vin Santo, mix well and leave to plump up for several hours or overnight. Alternatively, put the bowl in the microwave and heat on MEDIUM for 1 minute. Put the ricotta cheese, soft cheese and sour cream in a large bowl and, using a wooden spoon or electric hand mixer, beat well. Put the egg yolks and sugar in a separate bowl and beat until light and creamy. Add the cheese mixture and vanilla essence and beat until smooth.

Put the egg whites and a pinch of salt in a separate, spotlessly clean, grease-free bowl. Using a balloon whisk or electric hand mixer, whisk until soft peaks form, then fold into the cheese mixture. Spoon the filling into the pastry case and sprinkle nutmeg generously over the top. Bake in the centre of a preheated oven at 180°C (350°F) Gas 4 for 30–40 minutes or until golden but still a little soft in the centre. Transfer to a wire rack and let cool. Most cheesecakes may split when baking: don't worry, the split will contract on cooling. Serve at room temperature.

This is a delicious and simple cheesecake made in my grandfather's native county. Although he married a Scots lass and lived all his married life in Scotland, he still ate his apple pie or Christmas pudding with a wedge of cheese like a true Yorkshireman. He would have loved this cheesecake. You can make curd at home by adding a tablespoon of lemon juice to 600 ml freshly boiled milk, waiting until it separates, then draining off the whey.

yorkshire cheesecake

½ recipe Basic Shortcrust Pastry (page 9)

plain flour, for dusting

Filling

250 g curd or cottage cheese

2 tablespoons caster sugar

2 eggs

finely grated zest of 1½ unwaxed lemons and the juice of ½ lemon

2 teaspoons cornflour

2 tablespoons double cream

1 tablespoon melted butter

40 g raisins or currants, soaked in boiling water for 20 minutes

a deep pie plate, 25 cm diameter or a loose-based tart tin, 23 cm diameter

baking parchment and ceramic baking beans or rice

Serves 6

Roll out the pastry thinly on a lightly floured work surface and use to line the pie plate or tart tin, then chill or freeze for 20 minutes. If using a pie plate, make a decorative edge. Cut out a piece of baking parchment to fit the plate or tin and use to line the pastry case, then fill with ceramic baking beans or rice. Alternatively, line the pastry case with crumpled foil. Bake in a preheated oven at 200°C (400°F) Gas 6 for 10 minutes. Remove the baking parchment and beans or foil and return to the oven for a further 5 minutes. Reduce the oven temperature to 180°C (350°F) Gas 4.

Strain the curd cheese in a large bowl. Add the sugar, eggs, lemon zest and lemon juice and, using a wooden spoon or electric hand mixer, beat until smooth. Put the cornflour and cream in another bowl, mix to a smooth paste, then beat into the cheese mixture with the melted butter. Pour the mixture into the pastry case.

Drain the raisins, pat dry with kitchen paper, then sprinkle them over the top of the cheesecake. Bake in a preheated oven at 180°C (350°F) Gas 4 for 30 minutes until set. Let cool and serve at cool room temperature.

These were named after the ladies (maids of honour) who carried them back to Richmond Palace for King Henry VIII or Queen Elizabeth I – both monarchs, it is said, loved these little cheesecakes made by a local baker. I include a spoonful of best cherry compote or jam in the base of each – almond and cherry make a great combination. I like to make these in small, deep tins (like mini-brioche tins) if you can find them, as the filling seems moister and they look great!

little richmond maids of honour

1 recipe Sweet Rich Shortcrust Pastry (page 9, see Variation), at room temperature

plain flour, for dusting

Filling

50 g unsalted butter

75 g caster sugar

finely grated zest and juice of 1 unwaxed lemon

125 g curd or cottage cheese

2 large eggs, beaten

75 ml brandy or cherry brandy

125 g ground almonds

about 12 tablespoons cherry conserve

8 sprigs of rosemary (optional)

salt

icing sugar, for dusting

8 loose-based tartlet tins, 10 cm diameter

Makes 8

Roll out the pastry thinly on a lightly floured work surface and use to line the tartlet tins. Stand on a baking sheet and chill for 30 minutes.

Put the butter, sugar and lemon zest in a large bowl and, using a wooden spoon or electric hand mixer, beat until pale and fluffy. Strain the curd or cottage cheese into another bowl (do not blend in a food processor, otherwise the texture will be altered), then beat the curd or cottage cheese into the butter and sugar mixture. Beat in the eggs, lemon juice and brandy, then gently fold in the ground almonds and a pinch of salt.

Drop a spoonful of cherry conserve in each pastry case, then add the almond filling to about two-thirds full to leave room for rising. Bake in a preheated oven at 180°C (350°F) Gas 4 for 20–25 minutes until risen and golden brown. Remove from the oven and let cool slightly. Spear each cheesecake with a sprig of fresh rosemary and serve warm, dusted with icing sugar.

Note The cheesecakes may also be made in smaller, deeper tins, but will need a longer cooking time.

goats' cheese and ginger
cheesecake with rhubarb compote

This deep, creamy, mild cheesecake made with goats' cheese is spectacular when served with a stunningly pink compote of new season's rhubarb. As rhubarb and ginger are such a classic flavour combination, I've added ginger to the pastry and to the filling to give it a bit of punch!

Pastry

350 g plain flour, plus extra for dusting

225 g butter

2 teaspoons ground ginger

2 tablespoons icing sugar, sifted

1 large egg, beaten

5 tablespoons chilled Green Ginger Wine or sweet white wine mixed with 2 tablespoons very finely chopped stem ginger

salt

Filling

500 g soft goats' cheese

100 g caster sugar

vanilla essence, to taste

6 large eggs, separated

150 ml double cream

100 g glacé ginger or stem ginger, chopped

12–15 fresh bay leaves, to decorate (optional)

Rhubarb Compote

1 kg fresh rhubarb, trimmed

350 g caster sugar or to taste

a springform cake tin, 23 cm diameter

Serves 10

To make the pastry, put the flour in a large bowl, add the butter and rub it in until the mixture resembles breadcrumbs. Add the ginger, sugar, salt, egg and wine and mix to a firm dough. Transfer the dough to a lightly floured work surface and knead lightly, then wrap and chill for 30 minutes. Roll out the dough thinly on a lightly floured work surface and use to line the cake tin. Chill or freeze for 15 minutes, then trim down 2 cm from the top edge of the tin and discard the trimmings. Chill until required.

Put the goats' cheese, sugar, vanilla essence, egg yolks and cream in a large bowl and, using a wooden spoon or electric hand mixer, beat lightly. Stir in the chopped ginger and 2 tablespoons of syrup from the stem ginger jar, if using. Put 4 of the egg whites and a pinch of salt in a spotlessly clean, grease-free bowl and whisk until stiff but not dry. Fold into the cheese mixture, then spoon into the pastry case. Decorate with a ring of bay leaves (do this lightly, because they will sink slightly during cooking). Bake in a preheated oven at 180°C (350°F) Gas 4 for 20 minutes, then cover the top with foil (to prevent the bay leaves burning) and bake for a further 25 minutes or until well risen and dark golden brown. Turn off the oven, uncover the cheesecake and let cool in the oven for 20 minutes. Serve warm or cold (not chilled) with the compote.

To make the compote, cut the rhubarb into 3 cm chunks and put in a wide saucepan with the sugar. Cover and cook, stirring occasionally, for 10 minutes or until juices start to flow, the rhubarb starts to disintegrate and the sugar has dissolved. Taste and add more sugar if necessary. Transfer to a bowl to cool, cover with clingfilm and chill until required.

I first tasted this cheesecake on a trip to France, when luscious ripe red-centred figs were in season at the end of September. The contrast between the plain light vanilla cheesecake, crisp pastry and warm caramelized figs was a revelation!

caramelized purple fig cheesecake

1 recipe Sweet Rich Shortcrust Pastry (page 9, see Variation), at room temperature

plain flour, for dusting

Filling

3 eggs

125 g butter, softened

125 g caster sugar or vanilla sugar

225 g fromage frais

1 vanilla pod

8 ripe purple figs (the ones with the ruby red centres)

redcurrant jelly

salt

a loose-based tart tin, 20 cm diameter

baking parchment and ceramic baking beans or rice

Serves 6

Roll out the pastry thinly on a lightly floured work surface and use to line the tart tin. Prick the base with a fork. Cut out a large piece of baking parchment to fit the tin, use to line the pastry case, then fill with ceramic baking beans or rice. Alternatively, line with crumpled foil. Bake in a preheated oven at 190°C (375°F) Gas 5 for 10 minutes. Remove the baking parchment and beans or foil and return to the oven for a further 5 minutes or until just coloured. Put 1 egg and a pinch of salt in a small bowl and beat well, then use to brush the inside of the baked pastry case. Bake for a further 5–8 minutes until the egg is set and shiny. Cool in the tin.

Put the butter and sugar in a large bowl and, using a wooden spoon or electric hand mixer, beat until soft and fluffy, then beat in the fromage frais. Split the vanilla pod lengthways and scrape out the seeds with the tip of a knife. Put the 2 remaining eggs in a separate bowl, add the vanilla seeds, beat well, then gradually beat them into the cheese mixture. Pour the filling into the pastry case and bake in a preheated oven at 190°C (375°F) Gas 5 for 25–30 minutes until risen and brown. Let cool in the tin for 10 minutes, then transfer to a wire rack to cool completely.

Cut the figs into quarters and arrange on top of the cheesecake, making sure that they sit upright. Put the redcurrant jelly in a small saucepan, warm over gentle heat, then lightly brush over the figs. Cover the pastry edges with foil to prevent overbrowning. Put the cheesecake under a preheated grill and cook quickly until the figs start to 'catch' and brown. Brush with some more warm redcurrant jelly and serve immediately.

When I first visited Salzburg in Austria, I was amazed by the sweet cakes and pastries. I had never seen such a variety of strudels – all shapes and sizes, flavours and textures. This was one of my favourites. If fresh cherries are not available, use frozen ones, but drain them well before adding to the filling.

curd cheese and cherry strudels

12 sheets Greek filo pastry (which tends to be thinner than most other types)

100 g butter, melted

Filling

60 g butter or margarine

60 g caster sugar

2 eggs, separated

250 g curd cheese, strained

finely grated zest of 1 unwaxed lemon

½ teaspoon ground cinnamon

60 ml sour cream

250 g fresh cherries, pitted and quartered

icing sugar, for dusting

several large baking sheets, lightly oiled

Makes about 12

To make the filling, put the butter and sugar in a large bowl and, using a wooden spoon or electric hand mixer, beat until pale and fluffy. Stir in the egg yolks, strained curd cheese, lemon zest, cinnamon and sour cream, then fold in the cherries. Put the egg whites in a separate, spotlessly clean, grease-free bowl and, using a balloon whisk or electric hand mixer, whisk until stiff. Gently fold in the cheese mixture.

Keep the filo pastry sheets covered with clingfilm to prevent them drying out. Put a filo sheet on a clean work surface and brush with a little of the melted butter. Starting at the short side of each sheet of pastry, 2.5 cm in from the front edge, spoon about 2 heaped tablespoons of the mixture along the edge, keeping 2.5 cm in from the sides. Flip the bottom edge over the filling, roll once, then flip the sides inwards to encase the filling completely. Roll up like a cigar, brush with melted butter and set on a large baking sheet. Repeat with the other sheets of pastry.

Bake in a preheated oven at 190°C (375°F) Gas 5 for about 20 minutes, until the pastry is firm and golden brown. Let cool slightly, then dust with icing sugar and serve warm.

Note If you make the filling in an electric blender, the curd cheese need not be strained.

This is a very special cheesecake indeed. Make sure that the chocolate and water are melted together – the shock of adding the water later will make the chocolate thicken and seize.

chocolate marble cheesecake

1 recipe Chocolate Crumb Base (page 10)

a little melted butter

100 g white chocolate, grated and chilled, to decorate

Filling

150 g plain chocolate, between 60–70 per cent cocoa solids, chopped

750 g full-fat soft cheese (Philadelphia), at room temperature

250 g caster sugar

1 vanilla pod, split lengthways, seeds scraped out and set aside, or 1 teaspoon vanilla essence

2 large eggs

a springform cake tin or deep sandwich tin with a removable base, 23 cm diameter,

Serves 10

Press the Chocolate Crumb Base mixture in the bottom of the cake tin. Bake in a preheated oven at 180°C (350°F) Gas 4 for 15 minutes, then remove from the oven, lightly firm down again and let cool completely. Reduce the oven temperature to 160°C (325°F) Gas 3.

When the base is cold, carefully paint the sides of the tin with a little melted butter, then chill until required. Put the plain chocolate and 50 ml water in a small heatproof bowl set over a saucepan of barely simmering water. Stir occasionally until the chocolate is smooth and melted, then keep it warm.

Put the soft cheese, sugar and vanilla seeds, if using, in a large bowl and, using a wooden spoon or electric hand mixer, beat until soft and creamy. Put the eggs and vanilla essence, if using, in a bowl and whisk well. Gradually beat the eggs into the cheese mixture. Pour 250 ml of the mixture into a jug, then pour the remaining mixture into the prepared tin.

Stir the warm plain chocolate into the reserved cheese mixture. Pour the chocolate mixture in a wide zigzag pattern over the surface of the cheesecake, edge to edge. Draw the handle of a thick wooden spoon through the pattern, zigzagging in the opposite way so the mixtures are marbled together. Do not overwork, or the pattern will be lost. Keep it simple and the edges neat.

Bake for 20–25 minutes, or until the cheesecake starts to puff slightly around the edges but is still very soft in the centre. Carefully transfer it to a wire rack and loosen the edges with a very thin knife blade. Let cool slowly by putting a large upturned bowl over the cheesecake. When completely cold, chill for at least 3 hours before removing the tin. Remove the tin and spread the sides lightly with a very thin layer of whipped cream. Press the grated white chocolate around the sides. Cut with a hot knife to serve.

An outrageously rich cheesecake based on the delicious ingredients of tiramisù – coffee, mascarpone, chocolate, coffee liqueur and rum. A creamy rum and vanilla mixture is marbled through a plain chocolate, coffee and liqueur combination, then poured into an amaretti shell and baked.

tiramisù cheesecake

275 g amaretti biscuits, ratafias or macaroons

75 g unsalted butter

Filling

700 g mascarpone cheese or full-fat soft cheese (Philadelphia), at room temperature

150 g caster sugar

3 eggs, separated

30 g plain flour

45 ml dark rum

½ teaspoon vanilla essence

175 g plain chocolate

1 tablespoon finely ground espresso coffee

3 tablespoons coffee liqueur, such as Tía María

icing sugar, for dusting (optional)

a springform cake tin, 23 cm diameter

Serves 8–10

Put the biscuits in a blender or food processor and blend until finely ground. Alternatively, put the biscuits in a large plastic bag and crush with a rolling pin. Put the butter in a saucepan and heat gently until melted, then stir into the crumbs until they are well coated. Spoon into the cake tin and press evenly over the base and 4 cm up the sides with the back of a spoon to form a neat shell. Chill in the refrigerator for at least 30 minutes until firm.

Put the mascarpone in a large bowl and, using a wooden spoon or electric hand mixer, beat until smooth. Add the sugar and beat until smooth, then beat in the egg yolks. Divide the mixture in half and put in 2 bowls. Stir the flour, rum and vanilla essence into one of the bowls.

Put the chocolate in a small heatproof bowl set over a saucepan of simmering water and melt gently. Let cool slightly, then stir in the coffee and coffee liqueur. Stir into the second bowl. Put the egg whites in a spotlessly clean, grease-free bowl, whisk until soft peaks form, then fold half into each flavoured cheese mixture.

Quickly spoon alternate mounds of the cheese mixture into the biscuit case until full. Using a sharp knife, swirl the mixtures together with a knife to produce a marbled effect (do not overmix). Bake in a preheated oven at 200°C (400°F) Gas 6 for 45 minutes until golden brown, but still soft in the centre – cover the top if it appears to be overbrowning. Turn the oven off with the door ajar, then leave the cheesecake in the oven to cool completely. Alternatively, transfer the cheesecake to a wire rack and invert a large bowl over the cake so it cools slowly. When cold, chill for several hours before serving. Serve dusted with icing sugar, if using.

I used to make this for big parties – easy to prepare in advance and utterly delicious. Don't use a honey that is too strong or it will dominate the flavour – acacia or orange blossom is just fine.

honey hazelnut crunch cheesecake

Hazelnut praline

100 g whole unblanched hazelnuts

100 g caster sugar

Raspberry Sauce (page 63), to serve

Filling

200 g caster sugar

55 g butter, softened

500 g full-fat soft cheese, at room temperature

25 g plain flour

2 tablespoons honey

5 eggs, separated

6 tablespoons single cream

1 teaspoon vanilla essence

1/2 teaspoon ground cinnamon

1/2 teaspoon ground nutmeg

55 g light soft brown sugar

75 g hazelnuts, toasted, skinned and coarsely chopped

a large baking sheet, oiled

a springform or straight-sided deep cake tin, 25 cm diameter, greased and floured

Serves 10

To make the praline, put the hazelnuts and caster sugar in a saucepan and set over gentle heat until the sugar has melted. Do not stir.

When melted, increase the heat and boil until the melted sugar turns to golden caramel. Immediately pour onto the prepared baking sheet and let set and cool completely – about 1 hour. Break into pieces, then put in a blender or food processor and grind to a fine powder. Store in an airtight container until required.

To make the filling, put the sugar and butter in a large bowl and, using a wooden spoon or electric hand mixer, beat until pale and fluffy. Add the soft cheese and beat until fluffy. Beat in the flour, honey and egg yolks. Stir in the cream, vanilla essence, spices and half the praline.

Put the egg whites in a separate, spotlessly clean, grease-free bowl and whisk until stiff peaks form. Gently fold into the cheese mixture, then pour into the prepared cake tin.

Put the soft brown sugar in a bowl and stir in the chopped hazelnuts, then sprinkle over the surface of the cheesecake. Bake in a preheated oven at 160°C (325°F) Gas 3 for 1 hour, then turn the oven off, leave the door ajar and let the cheesecake cool in the oven for about 2 hours. Alternatively, transfer the cheesecake to a wire rack and invert a large bowl over the cake so it cools slowly. Chill for 2 hours, but serve at room temperature sprinkled with the remaining hazelnut praline. Serve with raspberry sauce.

refrigerator cheesecakes

Uncooked cheesecake mixtures are flavoured in various ways and set with gelatine. The mixture is usually poured into a prepared case or onto a base of some description, usually made from crushed biscuit crumbs mixed with melted butter. Sometimes sponge cake is used for a more featherweight effect. The flavours and textures are limitless, but a light hand is needed when whisking and folding in egg whites for an airy result. Most fillings are gently set, because too much gelatine can give a rubbery texture.

Loosely based on the mixture for Italian *panna cotta*, these silky smooth cheesecakes are easy to make, yet sophisticated. If you can't buy mascarpone, use thick clotted cream or double cream instead. The cream will be less rich but still delicious.

mascarpone biscotti cheesecakes

2 recipes Biscuit Crumb Base (page 9), made with Italian biscotti (*cantuccini*)

Filling

300 ml mascarpone cheese, at room temperature

300 ml double cream

thinly peeled zest of 1 unwaxed orange

125 g caster sugar

1 vanilla pod, split lengthways

60 ml milk

1 tablespoon powdered gelatine

6 tartlet tins, 10 cm diameter, with removable bases

Serves 6

Press the crumb mixture neatly into the base and sides of the tartlet tins. Stand on a baking sheet and chill until required.

Put the mascarpone cheese in a large bowl and, using a wooden spoon or electric hand mixer, beat until softened.

Put the cream, orange zest, sugar and vanilla pod in a medium saucepan and heat until almost but not quite boiling. Stir occasionally to loosen the vanilla seeds from the pod. Remove from the heat and leave to infuse for 20 minutes. When cooled, remove the pod and gradually whisk the flavoured liquid into the mascarpone cheese.

Pour the milk into another saucepan and sprinkle the gelatine over the surface, then heat gently until the gelatine has dissolved. Stir the gelatine-milk into the cream and mascarpone mixture, then strain into a small jug.

Pour the cream into the chilled tart cases and chill for several hours or until set. Remove from the refrigerator 30 minutes before serving.

This cheesecake is the ideal finale to a dinner party – bananas and hazelnuts, topped with pieces of caramel, always make a great combination. Serve with a delicious Toffee Caramel Sauce or even Hot Fudge Sauce (page 62).

banana caramel cheesecake

1½ recipes Nutty Biscuit Crumb Base (page 10), using hazelnuts

Toffee Caramel Sauce (page 62), to serve

Filling

100 g caster sugar, plus 100 g extra for the caramel shards

225 g full-fat soft cheese

2 eggs, separated

150 ml crème fraîche

3 ripe medium bananas

finely grated zest and juice of 1 unwaxed lemon

15 g powdered gelatine

75 g chopped toasted hazelnuts

a loose-based round cake tin or springform cake tin, 23 cm diameter, greased

a large piece of foil, oiled

Serves 6–8

Press the crumb mixture evenly over the base of the prepared cake tin, then chill until required. Put the sugar in a saucepan with 6 tablespoons water. Stir to dissolve, then heat slowly until completely dissolved. Have another 150 ml water ready in a jug. Bring the sugar syrup to the boil, then boil hard until it turns to an amber caramel. Quickly pour in the water – watch out as it will splutter. Stir over gentle heat until the caramel dissolves again, then boil hard until thick and syrupy. Let cool completely.

Put the soft cheese in a bowl and, using a wooden spoon or electric hand mixer, beat until softened. Beat in the egg yolks and crème fraîche. Put the bananas in another bowl and mash with a fork. Beat in the lemon zest and juice, then the cheese mixture. Stir in the cold caramel syrup.

Put the gelatine and water in a small heatproof bowl, let sponge for 5 minutes, then set over a saucepan of hot water and stir until the gelatine has dissolved. Beat the gelatine into the banana mixture. Set aside until the mixture is on the point of setting (starting to set and thicken).

Put the egg whites in a spotlessly clean, grease-free bowl and whisk until soft peaks form, then gently fold into the banana mixture. Pour into the prepared cake tin and level the surface. Sprinkle with the chopped nuts and chill for 3–4 hours or until set.

To make the caramel shards, sprinkle the sugar lightly over the oiled foil, put under a preheated grill and cook until the sugar melts and turns to caramel. Watch carefully or it can burn. Let cool, then break into shards.

Remove the cheesecake from the tin and transfer to a serving plate. Decorate with the caramel shards and serve with toffee caramel sauce.

A wicked, silky smooth uncooked cheesecake for a summer's day. Serve with a strawberry sauce laced with a little balsamic vinegar to bring out the flavour of the berries and to cut through the richness of the cheesecake.

strawberry and white marshmallow cheesecake

1 recipe Biscuit Crumb Base (page 10)

1 recipe Strawberry Sauce (page 63), to serve

Filling

275 g mini white marshmallows

50 g white chocolate, grated

60 ml milk

1 sachet powdered gelatine

225 g curd cheese or fromage frais

1 vanilla pod

100 g caster sugar

100 ml sour cream

2 egg whites

350 g small fresh strawberries, hulled and halved

a springform cake tin or loose-based cake tin, 20 cm diameter, lined

Serves 6

Press the biscuit crumb mixture into the base of the prepared cake tin (using a potato masher helps to flatten the crumb base evenly), then chill until required.

To make the filling, put 200 g marshmallows and the white chocolate in a heavy saucepan, add the milk and stir over very gentle heat until the marshmallows and chocolate have melted. Remove from the heat. Put the gelatine and 75 ml water in a small heatproof bowl, let sponge for about 5 minutes, then set over a saucepan of hot water and stir until the gelatine has dissolved.

Put the curd cheese in a large bowl, and using a wooden spoon or electric hand mixer, beat until softened. Split the vanilla pod, scrape out the seeds with the tip of a knife, then beat into the cheese with 50 g of the sugar, the melted marshmallow mixture and sour cream. Beat the gelatine into the cheese mixture, then chill for 15–20 minutes until it starts to thicken (this can happen quite quickly), but does not set.

Put the egg whites in a spotlessly clean, grease-free bowl and whisk until stiff but not dry, then whisk in the remaining caster sugar, gradually, spoonful by spoonful, whisking until thick before each addition. Gently fold into the cheese mixture. Spoon the mixture into the prepared tin and shake the tin gently to level the surface. Dot the remaining marshmallows over the top (they should completely cover the surface). Chill for 3–4 hours or until set.

Carefully remove the cheesecake from the tin. Remove the paper and transfer to a serving plate. Spoon the halved strawberries around the cheesecake and serve with the sauce.

This is a cheesecake inspired by a pudding my mother used to make when I was a child. Adding cream cheese to the original mixture makes it very luxurious.

raspberry fluff cheesecake

1 large ready-made sponge flan about 28 cm diameter

Filling

500 g fresh raspberries

50 ml raspberry and cranberry juice, or just cranberry juice

200 g full-fat soft cheese (Philadelphia)

100 g sugar

1 package raspberry jelly, 135 g, made up according to the directions on the packet

170 ml evaporated milk

2 large egg whites

a springform cake tin, 25 cm diameter, lined with non-stick baking parchment

Serves 10–12

Cut off the rim to level the sponge flan, then carefully slice the cake in two horizontally. Wrap and freeze one half for use another time. Using the base of the tin as a guide, put it on top of the sponge and cut round to make a 25 cm circle. Set aside. Line the base and sides of the tin with non-stick baking parchment, making sure that the paper doesn't protrude above the edge of the tin. Arrange 300 g of the raspberries in a thick layer in the bottom. Chill.

Simmer the remaining raspberries in the fruit juice for 2–3 minutes, then pass through a sieve (don't worry if a few seeds push through) to make a purée. Let cool completely.

Put the soft cheese in a bowl, add half the sugar, beat to soften, then gradually beat in the cold raspberry purée.

Cut up the jelly into squares and put in a saucepan with the evaporated milk. Heat gently, stirring until the jelly dissolves. Cool slightly, then gradually stir into the cheese mixture. Whisk the egg whites until stiff, then gradually whisk in the remaining sugar until stiff and meringue-like.

Beat 2 large spoonfuls into the cheese and raspberry mixture then carefully fold in the rest, making sure there are no large pockets of meringue.

Quickly spoon over the raspberry layer in the tin and level the surface. Tap the tin gently to settle the mixture. Carefully lay the reserved sponge on top of the mixture. Press in very lightly just to make sure it is touching the whole surface. Chill for 2-3 hours until set.

To serve, invert the tin over a serving dish and release the spring. Remove the ring and base. Carefully remove the paper from the sides and top and replace any raspberries that may fall down onto the plate. Return to the refrigerator until ready to serve.

This creamy cheesecake holds rivulets of real raspberry and chocolate sauces in a crisp chocolate cookie case. Alternatively, if your time is limited, you could fold fresh raspberries and grated chocolate into the cheese mixture instead of the sauces.

raspberry and chocolate ripple cheesecake

Biscuit Crumb Base

100 g butter

2 tablespoons soft brown sugar

250 g plain chocolate digestive biscuits, finely crushed

Filling

350 g full-fat soft cheese (Philadelphia)

3 eggs, separated

100 g caster sugar

1 teaspoon vanilla essence

200 ml double cream

20 g powdered gelatine

Raspberry Ripple

250 g fresh or frozen raspberries

50 g caster sugar

Chocolate Ripple

50 g plain chocolate

2 tablespoons double cream

a loose-based deep cake tin, 20 cm diameter, greased and lined

Serves 8

Put the butter and sugar in a saucepan, melt over gentle heat, then stir in the biscuit crumbs. Press the crumb mixture evenly over the base and up the sides of the prepared cake tin. Chill for at least 30 minutes.

To make the filling, put the soft cheese in a large bowl and, using a wooden spoon or electric hand mixer, beat until softened. Beat in the egg yolks and half the caster sugar, vanilla essence and cream.

Put the gelatine and 2 tablespoons water in a small heatproof bowl, set over a saucepan of hot water and stir occasionally until the the gelatine has dissolved. Keep it warm. To make the raspberry ripple, put the raspberries and sugar in a saucepan, heat gently until the sugar dissolves, then boil for 1 minute until slightly thickened. Press through a sieve and let cool. To make the chocolate ripple, put the chocolate and cream in another saucepan, heat until the chocolate has melted, then stir well and let cool until just warm, but still pourable. Beat the gelatine into the cheese mixture.

Put the egg whites in a spotlessly clean, grease-free bowl, whisk until stiff but not dry, then whisk in the remaining sugar, gradually, spoonful by spoonful, whisking until thick after each addition. Beat 2 spoonfuls of the meringue into the cheese mixture, then quickly fold in the rest. Put small spoonfuls of mixture over the base of the biscuit case so that they join up, then pour the raspberry and chocolate sauces in between the spoonfuls of mixture. Spoon in the remaining cheese mixture and pour again (keep any remaining sauces to serve). Swirl the mixtures together with a skewer to produce a ripple effect. Give the tin a shake to settle the mixture, then chill for about 2–4 hours until set. To serve, remove the cake from the tin and carefully peel off the paper. Serve in thin slices with any extra sauces.

I have based this on a beautiful pudding often seen in French pâtisseries. The pink-coloured base is covered with a deep purple-red, shiny 'lake' of set blackcurrant purée. Fresh blackcurrants are best for colour and flavour, but frozen and canned work very well if the fruit is out of season.

blackcurrant lake cheesecake

1 medium ready-made sponge flan case (at least 23 cm diameter)

Filling

600 g canned blackcurrants in fruit juice, drained and juice reserved, or 250 g fresh or frozen blackcurrants

75 g caster sugar

60 ml crème de cassis

350 g full-fat soft cheese (Philadelphia)

2 eggs, separated

200 g double cream

1 sachet powdered gelatine

Lake topping

50 ml blackcurrant juice (if using fresh blackcurrants)

1 teaspoon powdered gelatine

fresh blackcurrants, dusted with icing sugar, to decorate

a springform cake tin, 23 cm diameter, oiled

Serves 8

Cut off the rim to level the flan case, then carefully slice the cake in half horizontally. Wrap and freeze one half for use another time. Using the base of the cake tin as a guide, put it on top of the sponge and cut round to make a 23 cm circle. Arrange the sponge in the bottom of the prepared tin.

If using canned fruit, put the fruit, sugar and crème de cassis in a blender and work to a smooth purée. Press through a sieve to remove the seeds, then set the juice aside. If using fresh or frozen blackcurrants, put the fruit in a saucepan with the sugar and 3 extra tablespoons of sugar. Bring to the boil and simmer for 5 minutes until they burst. Transfer the fruit to a blender, add the crème de cassis and work to a smooth purée. Press through a sieve to remove the seeds and set aside the juice. Let cool completely. Set aside 2 tablespoons of either purée to make the glaze.

Put the soft cheese, egg yolks and cream in a bowl and, using a wooden spoon or electric hand mixer, beat well, then stir in the purée. Put the gelatine and 75 ml reserved juice or water in a small heatproof bowl and let sponge for 5 minutes. Set the bowl over a saucepan of hot water and stir gently until the gelatine has dissolved, then stir into the cheese mixture. Put the egg whites in a spotlessly clean, grease-free bowl and whisk until stiff but not dry, then fold into the mixture. Pour into the tin and level the surface. Chill for 3–4 hours until firm.

To make the lake topping, put 50 ml reserved juice, the reserved purée and the 1 teaspoon powdered gelatine in a saucepan and mix well. Heat until the gelatine has dissolved, then cool until almost cold and just turning to syrup. Carefully pour over the surface of the cheesecake, making sure it covers the top. Chill for a further 1 hour. Carefully remove from the tin and set on a serving plate. Decorate with sugared blackcurrants and serve.

These little cheesecakes are an updated version of an old English recipe often served in little glasses or cups. Using cottage cheese gives a grainy texture and the orange flower water a wonderful light orange flavour.

orange blossom cheesecakes

2 recipes Biscuit Crumb Base (page 10), made with almond macaroons or ratafias

edible flower petals, such as marigolds, for sprinkling (optional)

Orange Needleshreds (optional)

1 unwaxed orange

50 g caster sugar

Filling

4 eggs, separated

50 g caster sugar

finely grated zest and juice of 2 unwaxed oranges

15 g powdered gelatine

350 g cottage cheese, strained

300 ml double cream

2 tablespoons orange flower water

8 tartlet tins, about 8 x 2 cm, with removable bases

Serves 8

Press the crumb mixture neatly into the base and sides of the tartlet tins. Stand on a large baking sheet and chill until required.

Put the egg yolks, sugar, orange zest and juice in a small heatproof bowl and set over a saucepan of simmering water. Using an electric hand mixer, whisk until thick and foamy – do not let it get too hot or the mixture will scramble. Remove from the heat and whisk until cold.

Put the gelatine and 75 ml water in another small heatproof bowl and leave to sponge for 5 minutes. Set the bowl over a saucepan of hot water and stir gently until the gelatine has dissolved.

Put the strained cottage cheese in a large bowl with the cream and orange flower water and, using a wooden spoon or electric hand mixer, beat lightly, then stir in the melted gelatine. Gently fold in the whisked egg mixture and set aside in a cool place until on the point of setting. Spoon the setting mixture into the tartlet cases to look like a pile of clouds. Chill for about 2–3 hours until set.

If making the needleshreds, remove the zest from the orange with a sharp potato peeler (removing any bitter white pith with a knife afterwards). Cut the zest into long fine needleshreds. Boil the shreds for 1 minute, then refresh in cold water. Put the sugar and 100 ml water in a small saucepan and stir until dissolved. Add the shreds and bring to a rolling boil for 2–3 minutes, then strain and put on a plate to cool. Before they cool too much, separate them a little so that they don't stick together. Serve the cheesecake sprinkled with a few edible flower petals or orange needleshreds, if using.

This is a cheesecake for a buffet party. It bursts with juicy pieces of tangerine, and is very refreshing after a meal. For a really special occasion, try using tangerines or clementines ready-prepared in a liqueur and sugar syrup, available from specialist grocery stores.

tangerine and chocolate cheesecake

Base

100 g butter

225 g plain chocolate biscuits, crushed

swirls of cream, piped chocolate decorations and tangerine segments half-dipped in chocolate, to decorate

Filling

8 unwaxed tangerines

25 g powdered gelatine

450 g mascarpone or full-fat soft cheese

4 eggs, separated

175 g caster sugar

300 ml crème fraîche or sour cream

3 tablespoons Cointreau or Grand Marnier

a springform cake tin, 25 cm diameter, lined

Serves 12

Put the butter in a small saucepan, melt over gentle heat, then stir in the biscuit crumbs. Press evenly into the base of the prepared cake tin and chill for 30 minutes.

Finely grate the zest of 2 tangerines and set aside. Squeeze the juice from 4 of the tangerines and pour into a small saucepan. Sprinkle with the gelatine and let sponge for 10 minutes. Remove the flesh from the segments of the remaining tangerines and chop coarsely.

Put the mascarpone in a large bowl and, using a wooden spoon or electric hand mixer, beat until softened, then beat in the egg yolks, 100 g of the caster sugar, crème fraîche and liqueur. Heat the gelatine slowly until dissolved, then stir into the cheese mixture. Fold in the tangerine zest and chopped tangerines.

Put the egg whites in a spotlessly clean, grease-free bowl, whisk until stiff, then gradually whisk in the remaining caster sugar. Fold into the cheese mixture and spoon into the cake tin. Level the surface and chill for 3–4 hours until set.

Carefully remove the cheesecake from the tin onto a flat serving plate. Decorate with swirls of cream topped with a chocolate decorations and chocolate-dipped tangerine segments. Alternatively, pipe an irregular criss-cross pattern over the top of the cake with a little melted plain chocolate.

The subtle combination of coconut and lychee makes these individual cheesecakes irresistible. Creamed coconut comes in a solid block and has a good strong flavour – other types of coconut cream and milk will not give the same effect.

lychee and coconut cheesecakes

1½ recipes Biscuit Crumb Base, made with ginger biscuits (page 10)

thinly sliced kiwifruit, toasted shaved coconut and shredded stem ginger, to decorate

Filling

75 g creamed coconut block

75 ml sweet dessert wine, such as Moscatel de Valencia

3 tablespoons stem ginger syrup

2 teaspoons powdered gelatine

24 fresh or canned lychees

5 tablespoons coconut liqueur, such as Malibu

300 ml mascarpone cheese

3 tablespoons chopped stem ginger

2 egg whites

50 g caster sugar

6 loose-based tartlet tins, about 10 cm diameter

Serves 6

Press the crumb mixture into the bases and sides of the tart tins, then chill in the refrigerator until required.

Grate the creamed coconut and put in a saucepan with the sweet wine, ginger syrup and gelatine. Heat very gently until the coconut has melted. Do not boil. Stir well and pour into a blender.

Peel the fresh lychees, if using, and cut in half to remove the stones. Add to the blender with the coconut liqueur and blend until smooth.

Put the mascarpone cheese in a large bowl and, using a wooden spoon or electric hand mixer, beat until softened, then gradually beat the purée into the cheese. Stir in the stem ginger.

Put the egg whites in a spotlessly clean, grease-free bowl, whisk until stiff but not dry, then whisk in the sugar, gradually, spoonful by spoonful, whisking until thick after each addition. Beat 2 spoonfuls of the meringue into the cheese mixture, then fold in the rest. Spoon the filling into the prepared tins and level the surface. Chill in the refrigerator for at least 30 minutes. Decorate with kiwifruit slices, toasted coconut and shreds of stem ginger before serving.

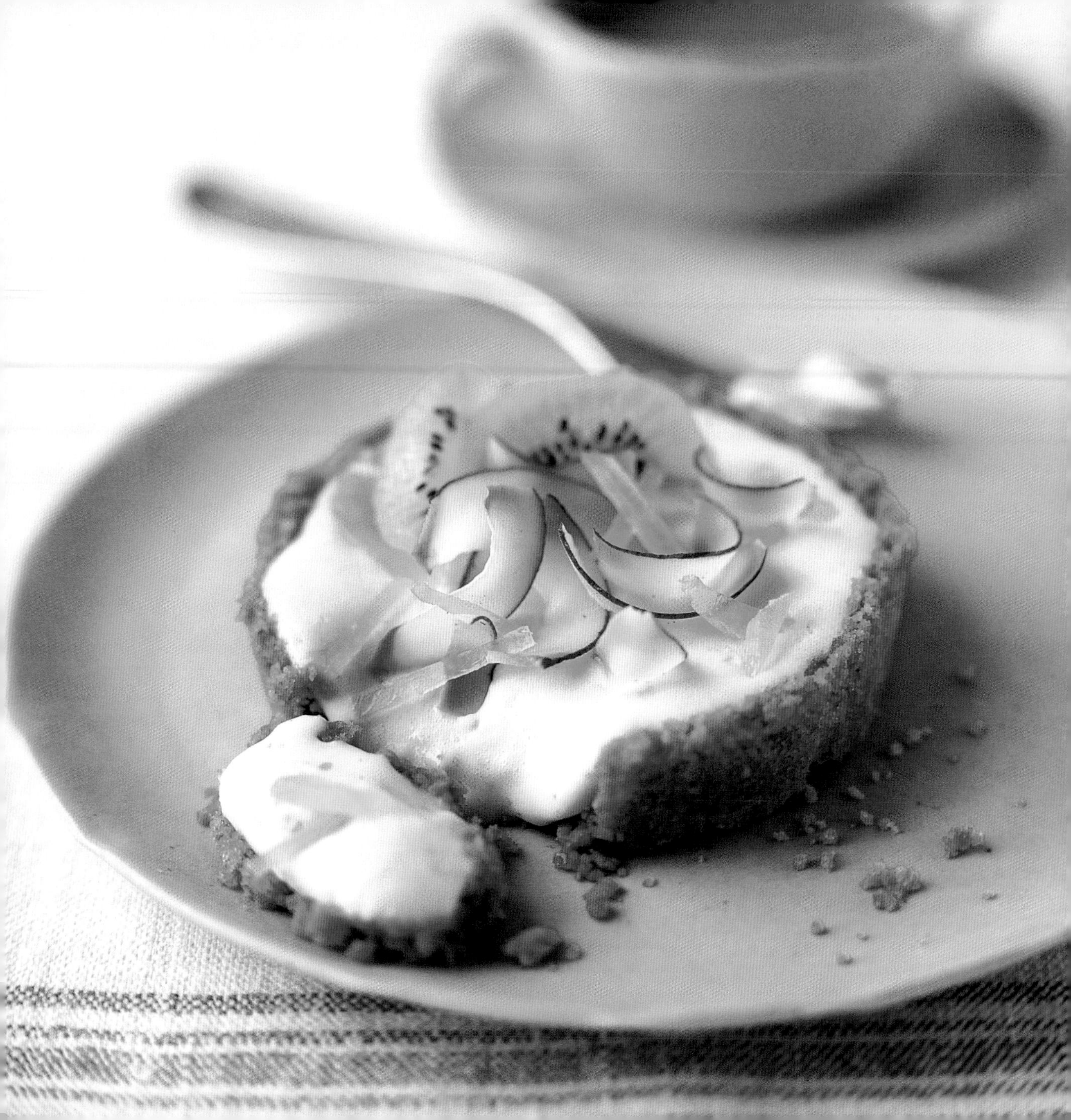

The tropical flavours of coconut, mango and passionfruit are given a lift with coconut liqueur and orange and lime juice. If you can't find canned coconut milk, use dried coconut milk powder and make up as for thick coconut milk, using the same quantity as in the recipe.

coconut cheesecake
with mango and passionfruit sauce

1 recipe Biscuit Crumb Base
(page 10)

Filling

400 ml canned coconut milk

1 vanilla pod

200 ml milk

4 egg yolks

125 g caster sugar

2 tablespoons powdered gelatine

150 ml mascarpone cheese

3 tablespoons coconut liqueur

1 large ripe mango, about 500 g

freshly squeezed juice of 1 orange

freshly squeezed juice of 1 lime

2 ripe wrinkled passionfruit

icing sugar, to taste

*6 deep metal rings, 6.5 x 6 cm
with capacity of 120 ml, oiled
(I use washed and dried food
cans, opened at each end)*

Serves 6

Stand the prepared rings on a baking sheet and press a layer of the crumb mixture into the base of each one. Chill. Put the coconut milk in a non-aluminium saucepan and whisk well. Split the vanilla pod lengthways and scrape the black seeds into the coconut milk. Stir in the milk, heat to boiling point, then remove from the heat.

Put the egg yolks and sugar in a bowl and whisk until pale and fluffy. Pour on the scalded coconut milk and stir well. Return to the saucepan and cook over gentle heat, stirring, until thickened like double cream. Do not boil, otherwise it will curdle. This will take about 15 minutes. Strain this custard into a bowl, cover with damp greaseproof paper and cool. Put the gelatine and 50 ml cold water in a small heatproof bowl and let sponge. Set the bowl over a saucepan of simmering water and let melt until clear. Stir occasionally, then cool slightly. Put the mascarpone in another bowl, beat in the liqueur to loosen it, then beat in the custard. Stir the gelatine into the cheese mixture. Chill for 15–20 minutes until the custard starts to thicken slightly. Pour into the rings and chill for 2–3 hours until set.

Peel the mango and cut the flesh away from the stone, then put in a blender with the orange and lime juice. Blend until smooth, then press through a sieve into a bowl. Cut open the passionfruit, scoop out the seeds, then stir into the sauce. Add icing sugar to taste. If the sauce is a little thick, add more orange juice. Chill. To serve, loosen the cheesecakes, slide each one onto a plate, remove the rings and spoon over a little sauce.

A wickedly dense cheesecake to serve with the coffee after dinner. It couldn't be any easier to make. You may add any liqueur you like, but my preference is for rum. Serve in thin slices, straight from the refrigerator so that it is as cool and firm as possible.

chocolate macaroon truffle cheesecake

1 recipe Chocolate Crumb Base (page 10)

mini chocolate dipped florentines, to decorate (optional)

Filling

250 g plain chocolate, over 60 per cent cocoa solids

300 g full-fat soft cheese

100 g light soft brown sugar

60 ml dark rum

100 g macaroons or ratafias, finely crushed

cocoa powder, sifted, for dusting

a sandwich cake tin, 23 cm diameter, with removable base

Serves 6–8

Press the crumb mixture thinly (you may not have to use it all) over the base of the cake tin and chill until required.

Break the chocolate into small, evenly sized pieces and put in a small heatproof bowl set over a saucepan of simmering water. Stir constantly, until the chocolate has melted, then set aside.

Put the soft cheese in a large bowl and, using a wooden spoon or electric hand mixer, beat until softened. Beat in the brown sugar and rum, then stir in the melted chocolate and crushed macaroons. Spoon into the tin and level the surface as neatly as possible. Chill for 1–2 hours.

When firm, dust the top with a thin layer of cocoa powder. Carefully remove from the tin (you may like to warm the sides of the tin to release the cheesecake) and set on a large serving plate. Decorate with mini florentines, if using, and serve.

A *semifreddo* is a pudding that is half frozen to give it a slightly thickened, creamy texture. Ricotta and mascarpone are sweetened, laced with rum and Tía María, and flavoured with pulverized Italian coffee and grated plain chocolate to give an interesting texture. You must buy very finely ground espresso coffee, or it will taste gritty!

1½ recipes Chocolate Crumb Base (page 10)

shards or curls, made from 125 g plain chocolate, melted, to decorate

icing sugar, for dusting

whipped cream, to serve (optional)

Filling

350 g ricotta cheese, at room temperature

350 g mascarpone cheese, at room temperature

1 tablespoon dark rum

3 tablespoons coffee liqueur, such as Tía María

1 teaspoon vanilla essence

4 tablespoons icing sugar

125 g grated plain bitter chocolate, 60 per cent cocoa solids

2 tablespoons espresso ground Italian roast coffee

a springform cake tin, 25 cm diameter, lined

Serves 6–8

coffee ricotta semifreddo cheesecake

Press the crumb mixture into the base of the prepared cake tin. (Using a potato masher helps to flatten the crumb base evenly.) Chill until required.

Strain the ricotta cheese into a bowl, then beat in the mascarpone cheese with a wooden spoon. (Do not attempt to do this in a food processor, otherwise the mixture will be very runny.)

Beat in the rum, liqueur, vanilla essence and sugar, then fold in the grated chocolate and ground coffee, leaving the mixture streaky. Carefully spoon into the prepared tin, leaving the surface coarse.

Freeze for about 2 hours until just frozen, not rock solid. The pudding should be only just frozen or very chilled. Transfer to the refrigerator 30 minutes before serving to soften slightly if too firm.

To serve, unmould, remove the paper and set on a large serving plate. Use a knife to cut through very cold plain chocolate to make spiky shards, then use to cover the surface of the cheesecake. Alternatively, to make chocolate curls, spread melted plain chocolate on a marble slab to a depth of 5 mm. When just set, draw a fine-bladed knife across the chocolate at a 45 degree angle to shave off curls. Dust with icing sugar and serve with a spoonful of whipped cream, if using.

Note Ricotta is a light fresh cheese made from whey. If unavailable, use strained cottage cheese instead.

sauces

chocolate sauce

75 g best-quality plain chocolate

50 g caster sugar

1 teaspoon cocoa powder

1 teaspoon vanilla essence

Makes about 350 ml

Break the chocolate into small, evenly sized pieces and put in a small heavy-based saucepan. Add the sugar, cocoa powder and 300 ml water. Heat gently, stirring occasionally, until the chocolate has melted. Bring to the boil and simmer for 15–20 minutes until syrupy and very glossy.

Remove from the heat, stir in the vanilla, then let cool. Reheat slowly to serve.

hot fudge sauce

50 g best-quality plain chocolate, 70 per cent cocoa solids

15 g butter

2 tablespoons golden syrup

150 g soft brown sugar, sieved

1 teaspoon vanilla essence

Makes about 250 ml

Break the chocolate into small, evenly sized pieces and put in a medium bowl set over a saucepan of barely simmering water. Leave for about 10 minutes until completely melted, then stir in the butter. Add 75 ml boiling water, stir well to blend, then stir in the golden syrup and sugar.

Transfer to a small saucepan, add the vanilla and bring to the boil, turn the heat down and leave to bubble very slowly for 5 minutes. Remove from the heat immediately. Keep it warm over the hot water, it will set as it cools. It can easily be remelted over gentle heat.

toffee caramel sauce

4 tablespoons golden syrup

2 tablespoons soft brown sugar

1 tablespoon unsalted butter

150 ml double cream

freshly squeezed juice of ½ large lemon

Makes about 300 ml

Put the golden syrup, sugar and butter in a medium saucepan and heat gently until dissolved, then boil until it becomes a rich golden brown.

Remove the saucepan from the heat, add 150 ml water, return to the heat and stir until dissolved. Pour in the cream and lemon juice, then boil until syrupy. Let cool. This sauce is best served warm.

strawberry sauce

500 g fresh strawberries

2 tablespoons icing sugar

1 tablespoon balsamic vinegar

Makes about 300 ml

Hull and halve the strawberries, then put them in a small saucepan with the icing sugar and 3 tablespoons water. Heat slowly until the juices start to run, then transfer to a blender or food processor, add the balsamic vinegar and purée until smooth. If you prefer, press the sauce through a sieve to remove the seeds. Pour into a small bowl, cover with clingfilm and chill until required.

Variation Make raspberry sauce the same way, but substitute raspberry vinegar for the balsamic vinegar – it just adds a certain sharp note to the sauce.

mascarpone cream

500 ml mascarpone cheese or double cream

3 tablespoons icing sugar

100 ml Italian Vin Santo or Marsala wine

Makes about 500 ml

Put the mascarpone cheese, icing sugar and Vin Santo in a large bowl and, using a balloon whisk or electric hand mixer, whisk until soft peaks are formed. Chill until required.

lemon syllabub cream

finely grated zest and juice of 1 unwaxed lemon

6 tablespoons Madeira wine or sherry

150 ml dry white wine, Madeira or sherry

freshly grated nutmeg

500 ml double cream

icing sugar, to taste

Makes about 500 ml

Put the lemon zest in a bowl with the Madeira, wine and grated nutmeg. Leave to macerate for at least 1 hour. Strain into another bowl.

Put the cream and icing sugar to taste in another bowl, and using a balloon whisk or electric hand mixer, whisk until just starting to thicken, then gradually whisk in the flavoured wine until the mixture forms soft peaks. Use immediately, otherwise it will separate.

index